EXPLORING THE STATES

Connecticut

THE CONSTITUTION STATE

by Emily Rose Oachs

BLASTOFF! READERS 5

BELLWETHER MEDIA · MINNEAPOLIS, MN

Note to Librarians, Teachers, and Parents:

Blastoff! Readers are carefully developed by literacy experts and combine standards-based content with developmentally appropriate text.

Level 1 provides the most support through repetition of high-frequency words, light text, predictable sentence patterns, and strong visual support.

Level 2 offers early readers a bit more challenge through varied simple sentences, increased text load, and less repetition of high-frequency words.

Level 3 advances early-fluent readers toward fluency through increased text and concept load, less reliance on visuals, longer sentences, and more literary language.

Level 4 builds reading stamina by providing more text per page, increased use of punctuation, greater variation in sentence patterns, and increasingly challenging vocabulary.

Level 5 encourages children to move from "learning to read" to "reading to learn" by providing even more text, varied writing styles, and less familiar topics.

Whichever book is right for your reader, Blastoff! Readers are the perfect books to build confidence and encourage a love of reading that will last a lifetime!

This edition first published in 2014 by Bellwether Media, Inc.

No part of this publication may be reproduced in whole or in part without written permission of the publisher. For information regarding permission, write to Bellwether Media, Inc., Attention: Permissions Department, 5357 Penn Avenue South, Minneapolis, MN 55419.

Library of Congress Cataloging-in-Publication Data

Oachs, Emily Rose.
  Connecticut / by Emily Rose Oachs.
    pages cm. – (Blastoff! readers. Exploring the states)
  Includes bibliographical references and index.
  Summary: "Developed by literacy experts for students in grades three through seven, this book introduces young readers to the geography and culture of Connecticut"– Provided by publisher.
  Includes bibliographical references and index.
  ISBN 978-1-62617-006-3 (hardcover : alk. paper)
  1. Connecticut–Juvenile literature. I. Title.
  F94.3.O215 2014
  974.6–dc23
                                                              2013011035

Printed in the United States of America, North Mankato, MN.

Table of Contents

Where Is Connecticut?

Did you know?
Nor'easters are storms that strike the Atlantic Coast. They can bring strong winds and heavy rains. Long Island Sound helps protect Connecticut from these severe storms.

New York

Stamford

Connecticut is located on the East Coast of the United States. This **New England** state is the third smallest in the nation. Hartford, the capital, sits on the Connecticut River in the center of the state.

Massachusetts

Hartford

Connecticut

Connecticut River

Rhode Island

New Haven

Bridgeport

Long Island Sound

Atlantic Ocean

Rhode Island borders Connecticut to the east. Massachusetts is its neighbor to the north. Connecticut shares its western boundary with New York. To the south is Long Island **Sound**. Connecticut and New York share this body of water. It connects to the Atlantic Ocean.

History

Native American tribes lived in Connecticut when Europeans first arrived. English **colonists** from Massachusetts built the region's first permanent settlements. During the **Revolutionary War**, American colonists fought for independence from England. The colonists won the war in 1783. Five years later, Connecticut became the nation's fifth state.

Did you know?
Nathan Hale is one of Connecticut's official state heroes. He is known for his love of America. His final words were, "I only regret that I have but one life to lose for my country."

Connecticut Timeline!

1614: Dutch explorer Adriaen Block sails up the Connecticut River. He is the first European to travel through the area.

1636: Settlements in Hartford, Wethersfield, and Windsor join to form the Connecticut Colony.

1701: Yale University is founded in New Haven.

1775-1783: Colonists fight British troops in the Revolutionary War.

1776: Connecticut native Nathan Hale spies on British troops. He is captured and hanged.

1788: Connecticut becomes the fifth state.

1833: Prudence Crandall opens a school for African-American girls in Canterbury.

1848: Connecticut outlaws slavery fifteen years before it is officially outlawed in the United States.

1941-1945: Connecticut produces airplane engines, submarines, and other war materials during World War II.

Yale University

Revolutionary War

war material production

The Land

The Connecticut River divides the state in half. It flows south through the Connecticut River Valley. Rich soil covers this broad, low land. The river empties into Long Island Sound. Miles of sandy beaches extend along this seashore. The coast has cooler summers and warmer winters than the rest of the state.

Trees cover the rolling hills that spread into eastern and western Connecticut. In the west, these highlands are part of the Berkshire Hills. They rise into the steep Taconic Mountains as they extend into northwestern Connecticut.

fun fact

More than 1,000 lakes are scattered across Connecticut. The largest, Lake Candlewood, is human-made.

Lake Candlewood

Connecticut's Climate
average °F

spring
Low: 40°
High: 59°

summer
Low: 62°
High: 81°

fall
Low: 45°
High: 63°

winter
Low: 23°
High: 39°

Traprock Ridges

In Connecticut's central valley, red cliffs tower over the lowlands. These are called **traprock** ridges. About 200 million years ago, **lava** pushed up through cracks in the valley floor. It cooled into hard, dense rock called traprock. Over time, the traprock **eroded** more slowly than the softer rock around it. This left giant ridges of traprock standing against the low landscape.

One side of these ridges slopes gently upward. The other side plummets to the valley floor, sometimes dropping 1,000 feet (305 meters). The iron in traprock rusts when it is exposed to wind and rain. This gives traprock ridges their distinct red color.

Sleeping Giant

fun fact

Some of Connecticut's popular landmarks are traprock ridges. They include the Sleeping Giant in Hamden and Talcott Mountain in Simsbury.

Wildlife

Connecticut is home to varied wildlife. Black bears roam through the northwest. In the woods, tiny chipmunks fill their cheeks with seeds. Cottontail rabbits leap up to 15 feet (4.6 meters) through brush. The five-lined skink is Connecticut's only lizard. Five white lines run down its back. Each winter, harbor seals **migrate** to Connecticut. These spotted sea creatures rest on the sunny beaches.

Brown bats flit through nighttime forests in search of insects to eat. Majestic bald eagles nest in tall trees. They hunt for fish along the coast. Great horned owls swoop silently through the dark night.

great horned owl

cottontail rabbit

five-lined skink

harbor seal

Landmarks

In New Haven, Yale University has some of Connecticut's best-known museums. Its Peabody Museum of Natural History houses a large collection of dinosaur-related items. The Yale University Art Gallery showcases masterpieces from around the world. In the east, the Mashantucket Pequot Museum and Research Center leads visitors through the area's history.

Hammonasset Beach State Park features a 2-mile (3-kilometer) stretch of sandy beach. Visitors bask in the sun and swim in the coastal water. The Appalachian Trail winds more than 2,000 miles (3,219 kilometers) from Maine to Georgia. It covers more than 51 miles (82 kilometers) of northwestern Connecticut. People can go for day hikes or camp along this **scenic** path.

Yale University Art Gallery

Peabody Museum of Natural History

AUDIO TOUR

SHIP CONTROL

PRESS 4

Hartford

English colonists built the first permanent settlement in Hartford in 1636. In 1639, the **Fundamental Orders** were adopted in Hartford. Some believe the U.S. **Constitution** was modeled after this document. During the 1800s, writer Mark Twain lived in Hartford. He wrote about the famous adventures of Tom Sawyer and Huckleberry Finn. His former home is now a museum.

Did you know?

For nearly 175 years, both Hartford and New Haven served as state capital. In 1875, Hartford became Connecticut's only capital.

Mark Twain's House

Today, many of the nation's **insurance** companies are based in Hartford. The city is also a major shopping center. Visitors to Hartford stroll the tree-lined paths of historic Bushnell Park. Some gaze at paintings in the Wadsworth Atheneum. It is America's oldest public art museum.

fun fact !

Southwest Connecticut is very close to New York City. Thousands of Connecticuters travel to "The Big Apple" for work each day.

In the early 1800s, Connecticut became an important center for **manufacturing**. Today, workers build clocks, silverware, and computer equipment. Factories also produce chemicals for cleaning products. Helicopters and submarines are manufactured for the military.

Most Connecticuters have **service jobs**. Many work for banks or sell property. Some also serve **tourists** at hotels and restaurants. Farmers grow flowers and plants for gardens. They also raise cows and chickens. Fishers haul in lobsters and scallops from the sea. Oysters and other shellfish are raised on fish farms. Near Hartford and New Haven, workers mine sand and gravel.

Where People Work in Connecticut

manufacturing
9%

farming and
natural resources
1%

services
78%

government
12%

Playing

The people of Connecticut like to spend time at the seashore. Some swim along the coast. Others hop on their boats to enjoy a day on the water. Fishers on Long Island Sound reel in bluefish. They also head to the state's lakes and streams to catch trout.

Connecticut's forests and parks allow for plenty of hiking and camping. Connecticuters ride their horses over the state's gentle hills. During the winter, snowy mountains are perfect for skiing. In larger cities, people attend symphony concerts to hear their favorite classical pieces.

fun fact !

In the 1920s, students at Yale University played catch with empty pie tins from Frisbie Pie Company. Many believe these metal plates were the first version of today's Frisbee.

Election Cake

Ingredients:

1 tablespoon yeast

1 cup milk, lukewarm

1/3 cup butter, softened

1 cup sugar

2 eggs, room temperature

4 1/2 cups all-purpose flour

2 teaspoons nutmeg and/or cinnamon

1 cup raisins

1/2 cup apple or grape juice

Directions:

1. Dissolve the yeast in the milk and set aside.

2. Combine the butter and sugar in a mixer. Beat eggs and add to the butter and sugar. Add the yeast and milk, mix well. Add juice.

3. Sift together 3 cups of flour and the spices. Add to the wet ingredients. Gradually add raisins.

4. Knead in remaining flour. On a floured surface, knead dough until smooth and elastic.

5. Butter two small loaf pans. Put dough in the pans. Let rise until doubled.

6. Preheat oven to 350°F. Bake 35 to 45 minutes. Cool on wire rack.

7. Top with light icing.

seafood
chowder

LOUIS LUNCH

fun fact

Customers at Louis' Lunch
know not to ask for ketchup
and mustard. The shop's
owners do not offer
condiments for their burgers!

Many Connecticuters believe their state is the birthplace of the hamburger. A New Haven sandwich shop called Louis' Lunch claims to have made the first one in 1900. The shop still serves their original hamburgers with cheese, onions, and tomatoes. Another Connecticut favorite is seafood chowder. Cooks make this creamy stew with clams and other shellfish caught in Long Island Sound.

Election cake is a **traditional** Connecticut dessert. Before the Revolutionary War, people gathered in Hartford to count election votes in the spring. Local hosts mixed up large cakes for out-of-town guests. Dried fruits such as raisins and apricots were baked into them.

23

Festivals

Washington, Stamford, and other Connecticut cities host maple sugar festivals every March. Festivalgoers learn how sap is taken from maple trees and turned into syrup. In 1973, seventy-two Japanese cherry blossom trees were planted in New Haven. Each April, people gather to appreciate the beauty of their blooms. Also in April, the Meriden Daffodil Festival takes place among 650,000 blossoms of this cheerful spring flower.

In August, people gather in Washington for the annual Green Corn Festival. It celebrates the crop's importance in the lives of Native Americans. The festival also features traditional Native American storytelling, music, and dancing.

maple tree tapping

Barnum Festival

fun fact

Bridgeport native and circus founder P.T. Barnum loved to put on a show. Now Bridgeport puts on an event to honor him! The Barnum Festival features parades, fireworks, and a ringmaster to lead the show.

Inventors

Over the years, many important inventors have made Connecticut their home. In the early 1800s, Eli Whitney found a way to make **interchangeable parts**. He built a machine that produced parts that fit in many guns. Before then, a broken piece needed a hand-made replacement. Eli Terry later became the first person to **mass-produce** clocks using interchangeable parts.

cotton gin

Eli Whitney

vulcanized
rubber

**Charles
Goodyear**

In 1839, Charles Goodyear
found he could strengthen rubber
with a substance called sulfur. Before this, rubber would
weaken in extreme heat or cold. His discovery allowed
rubber to be used in manufacturing. These and other
inventions represent the creative spirit and hard work
that continue to make Connecticut a great state.

Fast Facts About Connecticut

Connecticut's Flag

The Connecticut flag has a blue background. In the center is a coat of arms with three grapevines. The grapevines represent Hartford, Wethersfield, and Windsor. These are the three towns that joined to create Connecticut Colony. Under the coat of arms is Connecticut's state motto.

State Flower
mountain laurel

State Nicknames:	The Constitution State The Nutmeg State
State Motto:	*Qui Transtulit Sustinet*; "He Who Transplanted Still Sustains"
Year of Statehood:	1788
Capital City:	Hartford
Other Major Cities:	Bridgeport, New Haven, Stamford
Population:	3,574,097 (2010)
Area:	5,004 square miles (12,960 square kilometers); Connecticut is the 48th largest state.
Major Industries:	services, manufacturing
Natural Resources:	sand, gravel, soil
State Government:	151 representatives; 36 senators
Federal Government:	5 representatives; 2 senators
Electoral Votes:	7

State Animal
sperm whale

State Bird
American robin

Glossary

colonists—people who settle new land for their home country

constitution—the basic principles and laws of a nation

eroded—wore down by water and wind

Fundamental Orders—a 1639 document that explained how Connecticuters would be governed; it granted them the right to elect their own government officials.

insurance—the paying of regular sums of money for protection in the case of damage or illness

interchangeable parts—parts of the same size and shape that will fit into any machine of the same type

lava—hot, melted rock that flows out of an active volcano

manufacturing—a field of work in which people use machines to make products

mass-produce—to produce a large number of goods at once, usually using machinery

migrate—to travel from one place to another, often with the seasons

native—originally from a specific place

New England—a group of six states that make up the northeastern corner of the United States

Revolutionary War—the war between 1775 and 1783 in which the United States fought for independence from Great Britain

scenic—providing beautiful views of the natural surroundings

service jobs—jobs that perform tasks for people or businesses

sound—a long, wide extension of the ocean into land

tourists—people who travel to visit another place

traditional—relating to a custom, idea, or belief handed down from one generation to the next

traprock—hard, dark-colored rock that was created by lava

To Learn More

AT THE LIBRARY

Cunningham, Kevin. *The Connecticut Colony*. New York, N.Y.: Children's Press, 2012.

Garcia, Tracy J. *Eli Whitney*. New York, N.Y.: PowerKids Press, 2013.

Ollhoff, Jim. *Connecticut*. Edina, Minn.: ABDO Pub. Co., 2010.

ON THE WEB

Learning more about Connecticut is as easy as 1, 2, 3.

1. Go to www.factsurfer.com.

2. Enter "Connecticut" into the search box.

3. Click the "Surf" button and you will see a list of related Web sites.

With factsurfer.com, finding more information is just a click away.

Index

The images in this book are reproduced through the courtesy of: Enfi, front cover (bottom); Ffooter, p. 6; Pete Spiro p. 7 (left); North Wind Picture Archives/ Alamy, p. 7 (middle); Lebrecht Music and Arts Photo Library/ Alamy, p. 7 (right); Alan Copson, p. 8 (small); hd connelly, pp. 8-9; SuperStock, pp. 10-11; Enigma/ Alamy, p. 11 (small); Jamie Heimbuch/ age fotostock/ SuperStock, pp. 12-13; jurra8, p. 12 (top); Leena Robinson, p. 12 (middle); Nature's Images, p. 12 (bottom); FLPA/ SuperStock, p. 13 (small); Stan Tess/ Alamy, pp. 14-15; Chris George/ Alamy, p. 14 (bottom); ASSOCIATED PRESS, p. 14 (top); DepthofField, pp. 16-17; Philip Scalia/ Alamy, p. 17 (small); DVARG, p. 18; Tyler Stableford, p. 19; Peter Casolino/ Alamy, pp. 20-21; David Duprey, p. 20 (small); Freer, p. 22 (top); Planner, p. 22 (middle); M. Unal Ozmen, p. 22 (bottom); Foodio, p. 23 (top); Dmadeo, p. 23 (bottom); Phil Noel, pp. 24-25, Steven Valenti, p. 24 (small); wynnter, pp. 26-27; (Collection)/ Prints & Photographs Division/ Library of Congress, p. 27 (top and bottom); Anonymous/ Associated Press, p. 27 (top small); keerati, p. 27 (bottom small); Pakmor, p. 28 (top); hd connelly, p. 28 (bottom); eXpose, p. 29 (left); Shane Gross, p. 29 (right).